FEDERAL RESERVE INTEREST RATE

Steve k. Bryant

Copyright

Copyright © 2024 by **Steve k. Bryant**

All rights reserved. No part of this publication may be reproduced, distributed, or transmitted in any form or by any means, including photocopying, recording, or other electronic or mechanical methods, without the prior written permission of the publisher, except in the case of brief quotations embodied in critical reviews and certain other noncommercial uses permitted by copyright law.

Table of Contents

INTRODUCTION 5
   A Synopsis of the Federal Reserve's Function in the Economy 6
   The Significance of Interest Rates in the Financial System 8
   Goals and Purpose of the Book 10

Chapter 1 14
The Decision-Making Process of the Federal Reserve 14
   The Federal Reserve's Organization and Operations 14
   How Interest Rates Are Set by the Fed..............19

Chapter 2 25
The Rate Cut Decision Based on Economic Indications 25
   Important Economic Factors Affecting the Fed's Choices 25
   Examination of the Present Economic Situation 29
   The Significance of Inflation Easing but Remaining Somewhat Elevated 31

Chapter 3 35
The Federal Reserve and Political Neutrality........35

The Apolitical Position of the Fed in Historical Perspective 35

Chapter 4 46

Possible Repercussions for Various Sectors 46

    Debt from Credit Cards 46

    The Effects of Growing Auto Insurance 51

Chapter 5 57

The Environment of Savings 57

    Fed Rate Shifts' Effect on Savings Account Yields 57

    Online Savings Account Trends 59

    Expert Analysis from Sources Like Greg McBride of Bank rate 62

Chapter 6 65

More Comprehensive Economic Consequences .. 65

    The Effects of Fed Decisions on Global Economic Stability 65

    The Significance of Consumer Spending and Confidence 68

    Possible Long-Term Impacts on Important Industries 69

    Finance for Education 71

Chapter 7 74

Getting Ready for Changes in Finances 74

Useful Advice for Customers on Handling Rate Changes 74

The Value of Budgeting and Financial Planning 76

Resources and Tools for Taking Care of Personal Finances 78

Chapter 8 83

Prospects for the Future 83

Expert Forecasts for Upcoming Rate Reductions and Economic Situation 83

Summary of Important Ideas 92

The Wider Economic Consequences 94

Concluding Remarks on the Significance of Knowing the Fed's Decisions 95

Motivation to Maintain Knowledge and Take Initiative in Personal Finance Management 96

INTRODUCTION

A Synopsis of the Federal Reserve's Function in the Economy

The United States' central bank is the Federal Reserve or the Fed. Its main goal, as stated in the Federal Reserve Act of 1913, is to give the country a more secure, adaptable, and stable financial and monetary system. The economic panics that followed, most notably the Panic of 1907, demonstrated the necessity of central bank supervision over the monetary system to prevent future financial crises and led to the establishment of the Federal Reserve.

The Board of Governors, situated in Washington, D.C., and the twelve regional Federal Reserve Banks, dispersed throughout the nation's major cities, comprise the Federal Reserve System. Monetary policy is formulated in large part by the Board of Governors, which is a body that is confirmed by the Senate after being nominated by the President of the United States. The regional banks provide a range of services to the banking system and carry out local Fed policy implementation while operating with a degree of autonomy under the overall oversight of the Board.

Monetary policy, or controlling the amount of money in the economy and interest rates, is one of the main duties of the Federal Reserve. Three primary tools are used to accomplish this:

Open Market Operations (OMOs): These entail the open market purchase and sale of government securities. The Federal Reserve lowers interest rates and boosts economic activity by flooding the banking system with cash by purchasing assets. Selling assets, on the other hand, takes money out of the system, which raises interest rates and slows down the economy.

Discount Rate: This is the interest rate that the Federal Reserve will directly loan money to commercial banks. Bank lending increases when the discount rate is lowered because it becomes more affordable for them to borrow money, which stimulates the economy. The converse happens when the rate is raised.

Reserve Requirements: These are laws dictating the bare minimum of reserves that banks are required to maintain about deposits. Reducing reserve requirements allows banks to lend more money, which boosts the economy. Raising them can help cool an overheating economy by restricting credit.

Apart from setting monetary policy, the Federal Reserve also oversees and controls banks to guarantee the stability of the country's banking and financial sector and to safeguard customers' credit rights. In addition, the Fed controls systemic risk that could emerge in the financial markets and preserves the stability of the financial system. Additionally, it plays a significant role in running the country's payment networks and offers specific financial services to the public, financial institutions, the U.S. government, and foreign governmental entities.

The Significance of Interest Rates in the Financial System

A key element of the financial system, interest rates have a significant impact on many different areas of the economy. Interest rates are essentially the cost of borrowing money. They have an impact on how much money people, companies, and governments decide to spend, save, and invest.

Consumer Savings and Spending: Interest rates have a direct impact on how much it costs for customers to borrow money. Lower interest rates make it more affordable for consumers to finance large purchases like homes and cars by lowering the cost of loans for these kinds of things. This may result in higher consumer expenditure, which fuels economic expansion. On the other hand, loans become more expensive with increased interest rates, which can reduce consumer spending and slow down the economy. Savings are also influenced by interest rates; higher rates encourage more saving as opposed to spending because they provide better returns on savings accounts and other fixed-income investments.

Savings and Spending by Consumers: The cost of borrowing money is directly influenced by interest rates. Reduced interest rates cut the cost of loans for these kinds of products, making it more accessible for customers to finance major purchases like cars and homes. This could lead to increased consumer spending, which supports economic growth. Conversely, higher interest rates make loans costlier, which can lower consumer spending and slow down the economy. Interest rates also have an impact on savings; as higher rates yield better returns on savings accounts and other fixed-income investments, they promote conserving more money rather than spending it.

Control of Inflation: Reducing inflation is one of the main goals of monetary policy. Interest rates are a major factor in this. The Federal Reserve may raise interest rates to slow the economy by making saving more appealing and borrowing costlier when inflation is high. This lowers investment and consumption, which can lower inflation. On the other hand, the Fed may cut interest rates to encourage borrowing and spending to enhance economic activity and raise inflation to a healthy level when it is too low or the economy is in a recession.

Exchange Rates and International Trade: Interest rates influence exchange rates, which in turn affect international trade. The US dollar may appreciate as a result of foreign investors drawn to the country by higher interest rates who are seeking greater profits. A stronger dollar can narrow the trade imbalance by raising the cost of US exports and driving down the cost of imports. On the other hand, lower interest rates may cause the dollar to weaken, which would increase the cost of imports and decrease the price of exports thus widening the trade deficit.

Goals and Purpose of the Book

The goal of this book is to give readers a thorough grasp of the Federal Reserve's role in the economy, especially in light of the recent interest rate choices it has made. Interest rate decisions made by the Federal Reserve have a significant impact on both the overall health of the economy and the financial security of individual citizens. Readers can learn more about how monetary policy affects both the larger economic environment and their finances by investigating the mechanics underlying these decisions and their outcomes.

The Book's Objectives:

Inform readers about the role of the Federal Reserve: This book will give a thorough rundown of the Federal Reserve's composition, duties, and methods for influencing the economy. Gaining an understanding of the Fed's role is essential to understanding the decision-making process and reasoning behind monetary policy.

The significance of interest rates, their determination, and their wide-ranging consequences on consumer behavior, company investment, inflation, exchange rates, and financial markets will all be covered in this book. The impact of interest rate fluctuations on readers' daily lives and long-term financial planning will be explained.

Examine the Context and Implications of Recent Federal Reserve Statements and Decisions, Including Those Made by Chair Jerome Powell, in This Book's Analysis of Monetary Policy Decisions. It will examine the possible effects on the economy as well as the economic variables that drive these choices.

Provide Useful Financial Advice: Taking into account the effects that interest rate fluctuations have in the real world, the book will provide useful guidance for both people and companies. This covers methods for controlling debt, maximizing savings, and choosing wisely among investments in an environment where interest rates are fluctuating.

Prognosticate Future Trends: The book will also include professional analysis and projections regarding the state of the economy going forward as well as prospective Federal Reserve initiatives. This will keep readers up to date and ready for any changes in the direction of the economy.

Book Scope

The book is organized into various parts for ease of reading and comprehension, covering a broad variety of subjects linked to interest rates and the Federal Reserve:

The decision-making process of the Federal Reserve: A detailed examination of the Fed's decision-making procedures, including the functions and instruments utilized by the FOMC and Board of Governors.

Economic Indicators and the Rate Cut Decision: An examination of the major economic indicators—such as GDP growth, employment, and inflation—that affect the Fed's decision-making.

Political Neutrality and the Federal Reserve: An examination of the Fed's dedication to apolitical decision-making, particularly during election years.

Effect on Different Sectors: A thorough analysis of how changes in interest rates impact different sectors, such as savings accounts, mortgages, auto loans, student loans, and consumer debt.

Broader Economic Implications: A discussion of the Fed's policies in terms of financial market stability, consumer confidence, and long-term economic growth.

Getting Ready for Financial Shifts: Useful advice and techniques to help people and companies deal with and adjust to interest rate fluctuations.

Future Projections: Professional forecasts and scenarios about prospective actions by the Federal Reserve in the future and their effects on the economy.

By the end of the book, readers will have a solid knowledge of the Federal Reserve's function in the economy, the relevance of interest rates, and how these aspects interact to influence economic conditions. They will have the information and resources necessary to make wise financial decisions and maintain their resilience in the face of fluctuations in the economy. This book tries to offer helpful insights and useful advice, regardless of whether you are a student, professional, investor, or just someone interested in understanding the economic factors that affect your daily life.

Chapter 1

The Decision-Making Process of the Federal Reserve

The Federal Reserve's Organization and Operations

The core of the American financial and monetary system is the Federal Reserve, sometimes known as the Fed. It is the central bank of the United States. Its main goal is to give the nation a flexible, safe, and stable financial environment. Understanding the Fed's organizational structure and the several functions it performs within the economy is essential to comprehend the complexities of its decision-making process.

Federal Reserve System Organization

Various essential parts make up the Federal Reserve System:

Board of Governors: The primary governing body of the Federal Reserve System is housed in Washington, D.C. The Senate confirms the appointments made by the President of the United States to make up its seven members. The staggered 14-year terms that each member serves are intended to offer stability and continuity.

Although they have four-year tenure, the President appoints the Chair and Vice Chair of the Board.

Federal Reserve Banks: Situated in significant American cities such as New York, Chicago, San Francisco, and Atlanta, there are twelve regional Federal Reserve Banks. Although these banks have some autonomy, the Board of Governors maintains overall control over them. Every regional bank has a president and board of directors who manage day-to-day operations and offer insightful commentary on the state of the local economy.

Federal Open Market Committee (FOMC): In the Federal Reserve System, the FOMC is the principal policymaking body in charge of monetary policy. It is made up of five of the twelve regional Federal Reserve Bank presidents and the seven members of the Board of Governors, who are appointed on a rotating basis. Because the Federal Reserve Bank of New York plays a crucial role in implementing monetary policy, the president of the bank is seated permanently on the FOMC.

Member Banks: All commercial banks with national charters as well as numerous state-chartered institutions that choose to join the system freely are part of the Federal Reserve System. Although the stock in their local Federal Reserve Bank does not have the same rights as ordinary stock in a commercial company, these member institutions are still obliged to keep it.

The Federal Reserve's operations

The Federal Reserve carries out several crucial tasks to guarantee the efficiency and stability of the American economy, including:

Monetary Policy: Interest rates are the main tool used by the Fed to regulate the amount of credit and money available to the economy. The federal funds rate, or the overnight lending rate between banks, is one way that the Federal Reserve affects inflation, employment, and economic activity.

Supervision and Regulation: The Federal Reserve supervises and regulates banks to guarantee the nation's banking and financial system is safe and sound. Additionally, it seeks to uphold healthy financial markets and safeguard consumers' credit rights.

Financial Services: A payment system that facilitates the exchange of money between banks and the government is one of the many financial services offered by the Federal Reserve. In addition to serving as a bank for the US government, it also looks after the accounts of foreign organizations and other central banks.

Financial Stability: To avert and control financial crises, the Fed keeps an eye on and responds to threats to the financial system. It is essential to preserving the financial system's general stability.

The Chair of the Federal Reserve

One of the world's most powerful figures in economic policymaking is the Chair of the Federal Reserve. The duties of the Chair consist of:

Leadership and Representation: The Chair is in charge of the Board of Governors, acts as the Fed's principal public face and legislative advocate, and leads the Board of Governors. Financial markets and economic expectations may be greatly impacted by the Chair's communications.

Direction of Policy: The Chair is crucial to the development and execution of US monetary policy. They strive to foster agreement among the FOMC's members and direct its deliberations and decisions. The Chair's opinions frequently have a big influence on how policy is developed.

Economic Forecasting and Analysis: The Chair is in charge of the Fed's investigation and evaluation of current and emerging economic trends. This entails keeping an eye on metrics like GDP growth, employment, and inflation, all of which are essential for making well-informed policy decisions.

The Federal Open Market Committee (FOMC)

Setting monetary policy to support maximum employment, stable prices, and moderate long-term interest rates is the major responsibility of the Federal Open Market Committee (FOMC), the main policymaking body of the Federal Reserve System. The federal funds rate, which affects overall economic activity, is the FOMC's primary instrument.

Meetings and Composition: Five of the twelve regional Federal Reserve Bank presidents and the seven members of the Board of Governors make up the FOMC. The committee convenes eight times a year to discuss the state of the economy and financial markets, decide on the proper course for monetary policy, and evaluate threats to its long-term objectives.

Implementing policies and its tools: To carry out monetary policy, the FOMC employs several instruments:

Open Market Operations (OMOs): The purchase and sale of government securities in the open market to impact the supply of money.

Discount Rate: The interest rate that commercial banks pay the Federal Reserve when they borrow money.

Reserve Requirements: Minimum reserves that banks are required to hold against deposits.

Process for Making Decisions: Members of the FOMC evaluate different policy choices and talk about the state of the economy during meetings. They evaluate information on employment, inflation, economic growth, and other aspects. A majority vote is used to make decisions, and the chair is very important in facilitating discussion and fostering agreement.

How Interest Rates Are Set by the Fed

Since it has a direct impact on economic activity, setting interest rates is one of the Federal Reserve's most significant responsibilities. The federal funds rate is the main interest rate that the Fed manages. There are multiple steps involved in determining this rate:

Economic Analysis and Data Collection: The Federal Reserve is always keeping an eye on and analyzing economic data, which includes metrics like GDP growth, jobless rates, inflation, consumer spending, and company investment. This information helps the Fed determine whether its policy objectives are being reached and offers insights into the state of the economy as a whole.

Evaluation of Economic Conditions: Fed policymakers and economists evaluate the status of the economy today and project it for the future.

They take into account things like developments in the financial markets, fiscal policy, and worldwide economic trends. The premise for deciding on the proper posture of monetary policy is this judgment.

Policy Deliberations and Discussions: Members of the FOMC examine different policy options and talk about the state of the economy during meetings. They argue over how various interest rate levels might affect the economy. The objective is to come to an agreement on the course of action that will best support maximum employment and price stability.

Establishing the Target Federal Funds Rate: The FOMC establishes a target range for the federal funds rate following careful consideration and discussion. This rate has an impact on the overnight lending rates that banks charge one another, which has an impact on other interest rates in the economy such as those for business, auto, and mortgage loans.

Implementation through Open Market Operations: The Federal Reserve uses open market operations to reach the desired federal funds rate. This is adjusting the amount of money in the banking system by purchasing or selling government securities. The federal funds rate can be directed toward the target range by the Fed by modifying the quantity of reserves that banks have access to.

Communication and Forward Guidance: Through publications, press conferences, and remarks, the Fed disseminates its policy decisions as well as the reasoning behind them. Transparency regarding the Fed's policy aims and the management of market expectations are two benefits of clear communication. Economic behavior can also be influenced by forward guidance, which entails giving information about the anticipated future course of interest rates.

Recent Statements by Fed Chairman Jerome Powell

The Federal Reserve's current Chair, Jerome Powell, has been instrumental in establishing and disseminating the organization's monetary policy. His remarks shed light on the Fed's economic policies and decision-making procedures. From Powell's most recent remarks, the following are some major themes:

Regarding the Federal Reserve's independence

Powell has underlined the significance of the Federal Reserve's autonomy from political pressure on numerous occasions. He has declared that economic data and analysis, not political considerations, are the only factors used by the Fed to make decisions. This independence is essential to upholding confidence and guaranteeing the success of monetary policy in accomplishing its objectives.

Powell declared, "We never utilize our tools to promote or oppose a political party, a politician, or any political outcome." The Fed's resolve to stay apolitical and make choices that are optimal for the economy is reaffirmed by this statement.

Regarding the State of the Economy and the Prospects for Policy

Powell has emphasized how the Fed bases its monetary policy decisions on facts. He has pointed out that the Fed keeps a careful eye on economic metrics like GDP growth, employment, and inflation to gauge the state of the economy and choose the best course of action.

Powell has noted in recent remarks that inflation has significantly decreased, but he has also issued a warning that it is still relatively high. He has underlined that the Fed will monitor economic developments closely and modify its policies as needed to fulfill its twin goal of stable prices and maximum employment.

Powell has noted in recent remarks that inflation has significantly decreased, but he has also issued a warning that it is still relatively high. He has underlined that the Fed is keeping a close eye on the state of the economy and will modify its policies as needed to fulfill its twin goal of achieving maximum employment and stable prices.

Regarding the Labor Market

Powell has also addressed the job market, pointing out that a "normalizing labor market" is shown by low unemployment and a low number of layoffs. He has issued a warning, though, saying that the Fed is "watching carefully" for any indications of what could be a severe slowdown in the labor market.

This alertness is a reflection of the Fed's knowledge of the past correlation between economic cycles and labor market conditions. The Fed keeps a careful eye on employment data to foresee and minimize any economic disruptions.

About Lower Interest Rates and Economic Development

Regarding the prospect of interest rate reductions, Powell has stated that the economy would determine whether or not borrowing costs are lower, independent of political factors. He has reaffirmed that independent policy decisions are made and that political events, such as elections, are not taken into account in the Fed's economic forecasts.

Powell stated, "We would never attempt to base policy decisions on the results of an election that hasn't yet occurred." This declaration reaffirms the Fed's resolve to base choices more on economic principles than on political considerations.

The process by which decisions are made at the Federal Reserve is intricate and multidimensional, requiring careful consideration of the state of the economy, spirited discussion, and a dedication to independence and transparency. Comprehending this procedure is essential to appreciating how the Fed's policies affect the economy and, eventually, personal financial security.

The Chair and FOMC positions, the Federal Reserve's structure and operations, and the methods by which interest rates are determined by the Fed all play a part in the central bank's capacity to control economic activity and maintain financial stability. Recent remarks made by Fed Chair Jerome Powell shed important light on the Fed's monetary policy philosophy and dedication to remaining politically neutral.

This basic knowledge will be essential for examining how interest rate fluctuations affect different economic sectors and personal financial planning as we go deeper into the ramifications of the Federal Reserve's actions in the upcoming chapters.

Chapter 2

The Rate Cut Decision Based on Economic Indications

A detailed analysis of the economic factors influencing the Federal Reserve's policy decisions is necessary to comprehend the decision-making process of the institution. These indicators give the Fed the information it needs to evaluate the state of the economy and decide on interest rates. We will examine the important economic metrics that the Federal Reserve takes into account in this chapter, such as GDP growth, employment trends, and inflation rates. We will also examine the state of the economy today and talk about the importance of inflation decreasing but staying relatively high.

Important Economic Factors Affecting the Fed's Choices

A range of economic indicators are used by the Federal Reserve to assess the health of the economy and determine the best course of monetary policy. The Fed's choices, such as whether to raise or cut interest rates, are heavily influenced by these indications. Here, we examine a few of the most significant markers:

Rates of Inflation

The Federal Reserve's priority is preventing inflation, which is defined as the rate at which prices for goods and services generally increase and diminish buying power. The Federal Reserve's (Fed) goal of stable prices usually corresponds to an inflation target of about 2%. The following are the main indicators of inflation:

Consumer Price Index (CPI): The CPI tracks how prices for a market basket of goods and services have changed on average over time for urban consumers. It represents shifts in the cost of living and is one of the most popular measures of inflation.

Core CPI: This is the CPI that does not include the variable prices of food and energy. Because these erratic components are removed from the core CPI, long-term inflation trends are more clearly depicted.

Personal Consumption Expenditure (PCE) Price Index: The PCE price index tracks changes in the cost of goods and services used by individuals. Because it offers a more comprehensive estimate of inflation and takes into account shifts in consumer behavior, the Fed favors the PCE price index.

Core PCE: The core PCE does not include energy and food prices, much like the core CPI does. It is the favored gauge of underlying inflation trends used by the Fed.

Statistics on Employment

An additional significant aspect affecting the Federal Reserve's decision-making is the status of the job market. The Fed's dual missions include stable pricing and full employment. Important indices of employment include:

Rate of Unemployment: This indicator shows what proportion of the labor force is unemployed and actively looking for work. Generally speaking, a low unemployment rate indicates a strong job market.

Nonfarm Payrolls: This figure, which does not include the agriculture sector, indicates how many jobs have been added or lost in the economy. It sheds light on the state of the labor market as a whole and the ability of the economy to create jobs.

Labor Force Participation Rate: This figure indicates the proportion of individuals within the working-age population who are either employed or actively seeking employment. By demonstrating the number of persons engaged in the job market, it puts the unemployment rate into context.

Average Hourly Earnings: This metric shows how much an employee's pay has changed over time. An increasingly competitive labor market, where businesses are fighting for employees, maybe the cause of rising salaries and inflationary pressures.

GDP Inflation

The most comprehensive indicator of economic activity, the gross domestic product (GDP) represents the entire amount of goods and services generated in a nation. It is a crucial sign of the expansion and health of the economy. Among the GDP's components are:

Real GDP: This measure more closely represents economic growth over time since it is inflation-adjusted. It considers price level fluctuations and enables cross-temporal comparisons.

Nominal GDP: This metric captures the value of all goods and services produced at current prices without accounting for inflation.

GDP Growth Rate: This rate indicates how much the real GDP has increased or decreased over time. An economy is said to be expanding when its growth rate is positive; a contraction is indicated when it is negative.

Components of GDP: GDP consists of spending by consumers, investment by businesses, government expenditures, and net exports. Understanding the causes of economic expansion or contraction is made easier by analyzing these elements.

Examination of the Present Economic Situation

The U.S. economy as of the most current data shows a mixed picture, with several important patterns showing up in the examination of economic indicators.

Inflation

The Federal Reserve's top concern in recent years has been inflation. The economy saw a sharp spike in prices after a period of low inflation, which was fueled by elements including disruptions in the supply chain, increasing demand after the pandemic, and growing energy costs. According to the latest figures, inflation has decreased since its peak but is still rather high. Although the core and CPI have stabilized, the cost of some goods and services is still rising.

The Fed keeps a careful eye on the PCE price index, which has also shown signs of declining inflationary pressures, albeit not to the point where it would point to a return to the 2% target. Core PCE inflation is still over the target, indicating potential long-term underlying price pressures.

Employment

Due to robust job growth and a low unemployment rate, the labor market has proven resilient. Nonfarm payrolls have been rising steadily for some time, which suggests that job growth is strong. There appears to be a tight labor market because the unemployment rate has been close to historic lows. Still, there are indications of possible softening, including a deceleration in the rate of job growth and a marginal rise in the number of new jobless claims.

Although it has improved, the labor force participation rate is still below what it was before the pandemic, suggesting that some workers have chosen not to return to the workforce. The average hourly salary has been rising steadily, which is indicative of both rising labor rivalry and possible wage-driven inflationary pressures.

GDP Growth

Although uneven, real GDP growth has been favorable. Although growth rates have fluctuated throughout the quarters, the economy has recovered robustly from the setback brought on by the pandemic. A large portion of GDP, or consumer spending, has been sustained by high household savings and government stimulus programs. Additionally, business investment has increased, which has boosted economic development overall.

Nonetheless, several industries have encountered difficulties, including labor shortages and supply chain interruptions, which have affected output and economic growth. Due to problems with the supply chain and global trade imbalances, net exports have reduced GDP.

The Significance of Inflation Easing but Remaining Somewhat Elevated

The current state of the economy, in which inflation has decreased but is still rather high, poses a difficult task for the Federal Reserve. A thorough understanding of the variables causing inflation and any possible monetary policy ramifications is necessary.

The Reasons for the Increased Inflation

Supply Chain Disruptions: The COVID-19 pandemic produced severe disruptions in worldwide supply systems, resulting in shortages of goods and raw resources. These interruptions have continued, resulting in traffic jams and increased costs for a range of goods.

Demand Increase: Following the pandemic, economies experienced a sharp rise in demand from consumers, driven by large savings rates and government stimulus funds. Prices rose as a result of the constrained supply and rising demand.

Energy Prices: Increasing energy costs have raised inflation overall and have an impact on production and transportation costs. These price hikes have been made worse by shifts in the global energy markets and geopolitical concerns.

Labor Market Pressures: A tight labor market has led to rising pay as firms fight for workers. While higher salaries are helpful for workers, they can contribute to inflation if businesses pass on the increased labor expenses to consumers through higher pricing.

Implications for Monetary Policy

The Federal Reserve's principal tool for controlling inflation is altering the federal funds rate. In a scenario where inflation is falling but remains elevated, the Fed faces various considerations:

Balancing Act: The Fed must weigh the need to contain inflation with the risk of limiting economic development. Raising interest rates too soon could slow down economic activity and potentially lead to a recession. Conversely, not hiking rates sufficiently could allow inflation to persist, weakening buying power and economic stability.

Forward Guidance: It's critical to communicate the Fed's policy intentions. The Fed can manage inflation without making drastic policy adjustments by influencing economic behavior and market expectations through forward guidance.

Data Dependency: The Fed's actions are data-dependent, which means policy changes are based on the most recent economic data and trends. This strategy enables adaptability to shifting economic circumstances.

Inflation Expectations: Keeping price stability requires controlling inflation expectations. Businesses and consumers may modify their behavior in ways that contribute to inflation if they anticipate that it will stay high. The Fed wants to use communication and credible policy actions to ground these expectations.

Long-Term Factors

The Federal Reserve takes into account both the short- and long-term effects of its policies in addition to the current inflationary pressures. Persistently high inflation can be harmful to the growth and stability of the economy. The Fed's objective is to sustain maximum employment while lowering inflation to its target level.

Long-term structural economic changes, such as improvements in technology and modifications to international commerce, can affect the dynamics of inflation. The Fed keeps a close eye on these developments and modifies its framework of policies as necessary.

Economic data that are essential to the Federal Reserve's decision-making process include GDP growth, employment figures, and inflation rates. These indicators offer the information required to evaluate the state of the economy and choose the best course of action for monetary policy.

The U.S. economy is currently showing mixed results, with uneven GDP growth, a sturdy job market that may be slowing, and inflation that is dropping but is still relatively high. The Fed faces a difficult task in trying to strike a balance between promoting economic development and reining in inflation in light of these circumstances.

One cannot stress the importance of inflation abating but staying relatively high. The Fed must carefully balance long-term stability with short-term economic realities when making policy decisions. To fulfill its twin purpose of maximum employment and stable prices, the Federal Reserve modifies interest rates, issues forward guidance, and controls inflation expectations.

We shall examine how the Federal Reserve's actions affect different economic sectors and personal financial planning in the upcoming chapter. Gaining knowledge of these effects will help us better understand how monetary policy influences daily life and changes economic results.

Chapter 3

The Federal Reserve and Political Neutrality

The Apolitical Position of the Fed in Historical Perspective

Since its founding, the Federal Reserve's adherence to political neutrality has served as a pillar of its operations. The Federal Reserve was created as an independent central bank, free from direct political control, by the Federal Reserve Act of 1913. This allowed for the decision-making process to focus on economic factors rather than political ones when determining monetary policy.

Early Independence Foundations

Several financial panics led to the establishment of the Federal Reserve, most notably the Panic of 1907, which revealed the weaknesses in the American banking system and the requirement for a central bank to maintain stability. The significance of a central bank that could function independently of political influences was stressed by the framers of the Federal Reserve Act, which included influential individuals like Senator Carter Glass and Representative Robert Latham Owen.

The Federal Reserve System was designed with both public and private components to protect this independence. The regional Federal Reserve Banks, which have their boards of directors and receive input from the private sector, integrated private sector ideas while the Board of Governors, which is nominated by the President and ratified by the Senate, offered some kind of public oversight. This hybrid organization aims to strike a balance between autonomy and accountability.

Challenges of the Mid-20th Century

The Federal Reserve has encountered obstacles to its autonomy during its existence. For instance, the Fed faced pressure to maintain low interest rates during World War II to support the war effort, which resulted in the 1951 Treasury-Federal Reserve Accord. Through the termination of the practice of interest rate pegging to encourage government borrowing, this agreement reasserted the Fed's independence.

A time of severe inflation tested the Fed's independence once more in the 1970s. Despite strong political resistance, the Fed implemented an aggressive interest rate raise policy to combat inflation under Chairman Paul Volcker's direction. Volcker's resolve to put long-term economic stability ahead of political expediency served to emphasize the significance of an autonomous central bank.

Contemporary Times and Institutional Changes

The Federal Reserve has carried out several institutional changes in recent decades to bolster its transparency and independence even more. The Federal Open Market Committee (FOMC) was established as the primary body responsible for monetary policy setting, formalizing the process and shielding it from political influence.

The Fed has also stepped up its efforts to make its choices and policies more transparent to the financial markets and the general public. This involves providing advance notice of upcoming policy moves, holding frequent press conferences, and keeping thorough meeting minutes. These steps are intended to preserve the Fed's independence while improving accountability and openness.

Jerome Powell's Remarks Regarding Upholding Political Neutrality

Since taking office in February 2018, Jerome Powell, the chair of the Federal Reserve, has made a strong case for the Fed's political neutrality. He has continuously underlined the significance of basing monetary policy decisions on economic data and analysis as opposed to political concerns in both his words and deeds.

Focus on Data-Driven Decision Making

Powell has emphasized the significance of a data-driven monetary policy strategy on numerous occasions. He has emphasized that economic measures like GDP growth, employment, and inflation inform the Fed's choices in both public remarks and testimony before Congress.

For instance, Powell said, "Our decisions on interest rates are guided solely by our assessment of how best to achieve our dual mandate of maximum employment and stable prices," during a speech at the 2019 Jackson Hole Economic

Symposium. Political factors are not taken into consideration by us."

Reaffirmation of Institutional Independence

Powell has also reiterated the Federal Reserve's institutional independence. In times of increased political pressure, he has reaffirmed the Fed's independence pledge. Powell responded to inquiries concerning possible political sway over Fed policy in a press conference in 2020 by saying, "We never use our tools to support or oppose a political party, a politician, or any political outcome."

When the Fed took extraordinary steps to stabilize the economy during the COVID-19 epidemic, this dedication to neutrality was further highlighted. Powell insisted that the Fed was acting to boost the economy and fulfill its dual purpose despite intense political and public criticism.

Openness and Transparency in Communication

Powell has prioritized openness and unambiguous communication as a way to bolster the Fed's independence. Powell seeks to increase public confidence and comprehension by offering thorough justifications for the Fed's policies.

Powell emphasized the value of openness in a speech at the Economic Club of New York in 2021, saying, "Clear communication helps the public understand how we make decisions, which in turn helps to anchor expectations and contributes to the effectiveness of our policies."

The Federal Reserve's Strategy in Election Years

The Federal Reserve has particular difficulties during election years since there is a greater chance of political pressure. The Fed's strategy during these times is essential to preserving its efficacy and credibility. The Fed has historically done several things to make sure that its decisions are made with the state of the economy in mind rather than current political affairs.

Historical Models

Election-year moves by the Federal Reserve have frequently been closely examined for possible political undertones. The Fed has upheld the concept of policy continuity to dispel this impression by making sure that its decisions are in line with long-term economic goals rather than the whims of the political party.

For example, in the 1980 presidential campaign, despite strong political opposition, then-Fed Chair Paul Volcker persisted in his vigorous anti-inflation efforts. Volcker's position showed that the Fed would not waver from its policy objectives in the face of political pressure.

Strategies for Election Years

Data-Driven Decisions: During election years, the Fed gives data-driven decisions even more weight. The Fed can use objective standards rather than political sway to defend its policy decisions by depending on economic statistics and projections.

Improved Communication: During election years, it is even more important to communicate clearly and transparently. The Federal Reserve frequently steps up its attempts to elucidate its policies and the thinking behind them to the general public and financial markets. This strengthens the Fed's adherence to its dual mandate and allays worries about political motivations.

Sustaining Uniformity: The Federal Reserve endeavors to sustain uniformity in its policy measures and correspondence. The Fed can lessen the impression that the political calendar affects its decisions by refraining from making sudden policy shifts.

Interacting with Congress: The Federal Reserve communicates with Congress on policy decisions and economic conditions while upholding its independence. This interaction contributes to the Fed's accountability to the legislative branch and fosters confidence in its decisions.

Powell's Remarks During the Election Years

Jerome Powell has reiterated the Federal Reserve's commitment to maintaining political neutrality in election years in several remarks during his tenure. Powell once said, "We would never try to make policy decisions based on the outcome of an election that hasn't happened yet," during a press conference conducted in the run-up to the 2020 presidential election. Our dual mandate of achieving maximum employment and stable prices continues to be our primary priority."

Powell has often stated that economic circumstances and statistics, not political developments, are the basis for the Fed's decisions. With this strategy, the public and financial markets will be reassured that the Fed is acting independently and to foster long-term economic stability.

Obstacles to Political Impartiality

Even while the Fed is dedicated to remaining politically impartial, there are several obstacles in its way, especially when things are politically heated. Among these difficulties are:

Public View

Political rhetoric and media coverage can impact the public's perception of the Federal Reserve's actions. Political parties and candidates may examine the Fed's judgments closely and apply a political interpretation to them during election years. This may give the impression that the Fed lacks complete independence, even when its decisions are motivated by economic factors.

Influence from Politics

Particularly in election years, elected authorities may put pressure on the Fed to enact policies that support their political agendas. This pressure may manifest itself in the form of official declarations, proposed laws, or covert lobbying. The Fed needs to handle this pressure without compromising its commitment to making decisions based on data.

Uncertainty in the Economy

Economic uncertainty frequently occurs during election years, which can make the Fed's decision-making process more difficult. The Fed must strike a balance between the necessity of responding to immediate economic issues and the significance of preserving long-term stability since the economy can be unstable.

Techniques to Preserve Political Neutrality

The Federal Reserve uses several tactics to deal with these issues and uphold its political neutrality:

Institutional Defenses

The Federal Reserve System's organizational design offers protection against governmental sway. The Fed is shielded against transient political influences by the staggered terms of the Board of Governors, the rotation of regional bank presidents on the FOMC, and the long-term appointments of Fed officials.

Unambiguous Mandates

The Fed's two mandates—stable prices and maximum employment—provide a defined framework within which it can make policy decisions. By concentrating on these goals, the Fed may use economic standards rather than political ones to support its decisions.

Open and Honest Communication

One of the most important tactics for preserving political neutrality is open communication. The Fed can reduce public suspicions about political motivations and foster public trust by clearly outlining its policies and the thinking underlying them.

Interaction with Interest Groups

The public, financial markets, Congress, and other stakeholders are among the many groups with whom the Fed interacts. By increasing transparency and accountability, this involvement strengthens the independence of the Fed.

For the Federal Reserve to continue to be credible and effective in implementing monetary policy, it must remain politically neutral. Given the Fed's historical background and the remarks made by its current Chair, Jerome Powell, it is crucial to base judgments on economic information rather than political concerns.

The Fed faces particular difficulties during election years, but it uses tactics like data-driven decision-making, improved communication, and consistency maintenance to preserve its independence. Despite these initiatives, the Fed still has to constantly balance political pressure and public opinion to make sure that its activities are still directed at advancing long-term economic stability.

We will examine how the Federal Reserve's interest rate decisions affect different economic sectors and personal financial planning in the following chapter. Knowing these effects will give important insights into how monetary policy influences our daily lives and shapes economic outcomes.

Chapter 4

Possible Repercussions for Various Sectors

The decisions made by the Federal Reserve on interest rates have a significant impact on several different economic sectors. The possible effects of fluctuating interest rates on credit card debt, mortgage rates, auto loans, and student loans are explored in detail in this chapter. Making informed financial decisions and navigating the economic landscape more effectively can be achieved by individuals and enterprises by being aware of these effects.

Debt from Credit Cards

The prime rate, which is determined by the Federal Reserve's policy choices, is the basis for most credit cards' variable interest rates, which make credit card debt extremely susceptible to fluctuations in interest rates. Higher interest rates on credit card balances result from an increase in the prime rate, which usually happens when the Fed raises interest rates.

Techniques for Handling Credit Card Debt in the Face of Shifting Interest Rates

Balance Transfer Credit Cards: Moving high-interest debt to a card with an introductory 0% APR for a predetermined amount of time is a useful tactic for controlling credit card debt. By doing this, debtors may be able to reduce their interest rates temporarily and accelerate principal repayment. To prevent higher rates, it is imperative to pay off the remaining amount before the conclusion of the introductory term.

Personal Loans: Combining credit card debt with a low-interest personal loan is an additional tactic. Fixed interest rates are common on personal loans, which may result in more predictable monthly payments and possibly reduced total interest expenses. This method, which combines several payments into one, can make managing debt easier.

Dispute Resolution with Credit Card Issuers: Customers may also get in touch with their credit card companies to negotiate a reduced interest rate. Some issuers could be open to lowering rates for loyal customers with spotless payment records, however this is not a given. "It never hurts to ask," says financial analyst Matt Schulz, since many cardholders are unaware that issuers may grant such requests.

Debt Management Plans: Enrolling in a debt management plan (DMP) offered by a nonprofit credit counseling organization might be helpful for individuals who are having significant financial difficulties. In these plans, creditors are frequently persuaded to accept reduced interest rates and fees in exchange for combining payments into a single, monthly payment to the counseling center.

Advice from Financial Experts such as Matt Schulz

The chief credit analyst at LendingTree, Matt Schulz, highlights the value of proactive debt management. To save money on interest, he suggests that customers take advantage of balance transfer offers and personal loans. Along with emphasizing the importance of negotiating, Schulz notes that "many people are surprised to find that a simple phone call can result in a lower interest rate."

To reduce principle more quickly, Schulz advises giving high-interest debt priority and paying more than the required minimum each month. To guarantee regular, on-time payments, he also advises setting up automated payments. This can lower the chance of late fees and enhance credit scores.

Mortgage Rates

Numerous factors, including the state of the economy, the demand for mortgage-backed securities on the market, and the Federal Reserve's interest rate choices, all have an impact on mortgage rates. Mortgage rates often rise in tandem with increases in interest rates by the Federal Reserve, while other factors may also be important.

Present Patterns and Prospective Anticipations

Due to changes in Fed policy, worldwide events like the COVID-19 pandemic, and economic concerns, mortgage rates have fluctuated significantly in recent years. Mortgage rates have been historically low as of the most current statistics, but as the Fed works to normalize monetary policy, incremental rises are anticipated.

Lending Tree senior economist Jacob Channel says, "If we continue to get good news on things like inflation, mortgage rates could continue trending downward." However, he also warns that "we shouldn't expect any gargantuan drops in the immediate future, but we might see rates trending back to their 2024 lows over the coming weeks and months."

Techniques for Both Homeowners and Purchasers

Locking in Rates: Preventing future rate hikes can be achieved by prospective homeowners by locking in a mortgage rate at a discounted rate. Rate lock options are available from many lenders and might be helpful in a situation where rates are rising.

Refinancing: To benefit from lower rates, homeowners who currently have mortgages may want to consider refinancing. Refinancing might result in lower interest rates overall and in smaller monthly payments. To make sure that the potential savings exceed these expenditures, it is crucial to take into account the refinancing-related charges, such as closing fees.

Adjustable-Rate Mortgages (ARMs): While fixed-rate mortgages are stable, adjustable-rate mortgages (ARMs) may have lower introductory rates. Borrowers who intend to sell or refinance before the rate changes may find that ARMs are advantageous. It is vital to comprehend the possibility of future rate hikes and confirm that the borrower has the financial capacity to make larger payments in the event of an increase in rates.

Increasing Credit Scores: Mortgage rates are often lower for those who have higher credit scores. Encouraging debt reduction and regular payments are two ways to raise credit ratings, which can help you get a better mortgage.

Budgeting for Higher Payments: It's a good idea to account for the possibility of higher monthly payments if you anticipate higher mortgage rates in the future. To cover rising housing prices, entails putting aside more money and cutting back on discretionary expenditure.

Vehicle Loans

Another industry impacted by interest rate increases is auto or vehicle loans. Auto loans, in contrast to credit cards, usually have fixed interest rates, which means that the rate decided upon at the time of purchase is the same for the term of the loan. However, as interest rates rise, new auto loans may end up costing more.

Increased Interest Rates' Impact on Auto Loan Payments

For new auto loans, higher interest rates may result in larger monthly payments. For instance, the monthly payment for a borrower with a $30,000 auto loan with a 5-year term and a 3% interest rate would be about $539. The monthly payment will climb to around $566 if the interest rate rises to 5%. Even though the monthly difference might not seem like much, throughout the loan, it can add up to be quite a bit.

The Effects of Growing Auto Insurance

The cost of auto loans has increased due to growing car costs as well as interest rates. The cost of cars has increased due to several factors, including supply chain interruptions, rising demand, and shortages of essential parts like semiconductor chips. Many consumers now find it more difficult to afford auto finance due to the combination of rising prices and interest rates.

Methods for Controlling the Cost of Auto Loans

Comparing Rates: Similar to mortgages, you may save a lot of money by comparing rates on auto loans. To locate the best rates, customers should evaluate offers from several lenders, including as banks, credit unions, and online lenders.

Examining Loan Terms: Extended loan durations can lower monthly payments, but they frequently lead to greater overall interest expenses. It's critical to strike a balance between total cost and monthly affordability and select a loan term that suits the borrower's financial circumstances.

Down Payments: Making a bigger down payment can reduce the principal amount financed and, as a result, the total interest paid throughout the term of the loan. Additionally, by improving the borrower's loan-to-value ratio and lowering monthly payments, this may lead to better loan terms.

Leasing as an Option: For people who would prefer not to buy a car entirely, leasing an automobile can be a more cost-effective choice. When compared to buying, leasing usually has lower monthly payments; however, there are certain limits, such as mileage restrictions.

Examining Used Cars: With the cost of new cars on the rise, buying a used automobile can be a more affordable option. Because of the lower purchase price, used car loans typically have lower overall costs even if their interest rates can be higher than those for new cars.

Student Debt or Loan

Interest rate fluctuations have an impact on student loans as well, especially private student loans. Private student loans frequently have variable interest rates linked to benchmarks like the prime rate or the London Interbank Offered Rate (LIBOR), in contrast to federal student loans, which normally have fixed rates set by the government.

How Private Student Loans Are Affected by Variable Rates

Variable-rate student loans may change in value over time, resulting in adjustments to interest rates and monthly payments. The benchmarks to which variable-rate loans are attached typically rise in response to an interest rate hike from the Federal Reserve, which raises loan payments.

Relationship Between Prime Rates and Student Loan Interest

Many private student loans are based on the prime rate, which is determined by the federal funds rate of the Federal Reserve. The interest rates on loans that are linked to the prime rate increase along with it. For instance, if the prime rate rises from 3.25% to 3.75% and a private student loan has an interest rate of "prime + 2%," the loan's interest rate will climb from 5.25% to 5.75%.

Techniques for Controlling the Cost of Student Loans

Refinancing: To lock in a consistent interest rate, borrowers with variable-rate student loans might want to think about refinancing into a fixed-rate loan. This can guard against future rate hikes and give monthly payments some stability.

Making Additional Payments: You can shorten the loan term and lower the total amount of interest paid by making additional principal payments. Because it lessens the impact of prospective rate increases in the future, this method works especially well for variable-rate loans.

Using Rate limits: The maximum interest rate that can be charged on certain variable-rate loans is limited by rate limits. In order to appreciate these restrictions and how they can offer some protection against rising rates, borrowers should study the conditions of their loans.

Examining Federal Loan Possibilities: Before applying for private loans, students and families should investigate their possibilities for federal student loans, which usually have fixed interest rates and better payback conditions.

Income-Driven Repayment Plans: Income-driven repayment plans, which cap monthly payments at a proportion of discretionary income, can assist in managing payments for federal student loans. Although this has no direct impact on private loans, it can offer general financial relief and free up additional funds for debtors to use to settle their private loan debt.

The economy as a whole is significantly impacted by the Federal Reserve's decisions about interest rates, which have an impact on everything from credit card debt to mortgage rates, auto loans, and student loans. Individuals and enterprises can overcome the obstacles presented by shifting interest rates by being aware of these effects and implementing the necessary measures.

Rising rates can be lessened by using credit card debt management techniques like balance transfers, personal loans, and discussions with issuers. Refinancing, rate locking, and credit score enhancement are important cost-control measures in the mortgage market. Comparing rates, taking into account the conditions of the loan, and increasing your down payment can all help you save money overall when it comes to auto loans. Lastly, there is financial relief available for student loans through refinancing, additional payments, and investigating federal loan choices.

People can better manage their financial responsibilities and seize opportunities in a changing economic climate by being proactive and knowledgeable.

Chapter 5

The Environment of Savings

The world of savings is greatly impacted by the Federal Reserve's interest rate policies, which have an impact on everything from money market accounts and certificates of deposit (CDs) to conventional savings accounts. This chapter looks at trends in online savings accounts, the effect of Fed rate changes on savings account rates and offers insight from financial experts including Greg McBride of Bankrate.com.

Fed Rate Shifts' Effect on Savings Account Yields

The interest rate at which banks lend to one another overnight is known as the target federal funds rate, and it is determined by the Federal Reserve. A large number of interest rates, including those on savings accounts, are indirectly influenced by this rate. Banks usually boost the interest rates they provide on savings accounts to draw in additional deposits when the Federal Reserve boosts the federal funds rate. On the other hand, banks tend to lower savings account yields when the Fed declines.

The Impact of Fed Rate Hikes on Savings Accounts

Increased Yields: Banks typically respond to increases in interest rates by raising the yields on savings accounts. This is due to the fact that higher rates increase the cost of borrowing, which forces banks to provide more alluring interest rates on deposits in order to guarantee they have enough money to make loans.

Competition amongst Banks: A rise in the federal funds rate may encourage banks to compete with one another for client deposits. Banks may provide promotional rates or unique savings products with greater yields to draw in more savers. Customers stand to gain from this competitive climate by receiving higher returns on their savings.

Lag in Adjustments: It's crucial to remember that banks may take longer to modify their savings account rates once the Fed raises interest rates.Some banks make changes quickly to offer higher yields, while others may take weeks or even months to do so.

The Impact of Fed Rate Reductions on Savings Accounts

Diminished Yields: Banks typically give lower interest rates on savings accounts in response to Federal Reserve interest rate reductions. This is so that banks have less incentive to draw in deposits with high yields as lower rates make borrowing less expensive.

Diminished Incentives: Because traditional savings accounts yield less returns, savers may find it less alluring to put their money in them during times of low interest rates. This may cause people to look for alternative investment opportunities with better rates.

Rate Stability: Even when the Fed reduces interest rates, certain banks may continue to offer savings account holders consistent interest rates. These banks might provide stable returns, even if they aren't the highest on the market, to keep consumers.

Online Savings Account Trends

Since online savings accounts sometimes offer better returns than traditional brick-and-mortar bank accounts, they have become more and more popular in recent years. The emergence of fintech firms and banks that operate exclusively online has completely changed the savings market by giving customers additional options and competitive interest rates.

Benefits of Savings Accounts Online

Higher Interest Rates: Online banks can provide higher interest rates on savings accounts because they often have lower overhead costs than traditional banks. Because of this, many looking for higher returns are finding online savings accounts to be an appealing choice.

Convenience and accessibility: Having an online savings account allows you to manage your money from any location with an internet connection. It's simple to set up automatic deposits, transfer money, and check balances with mobile apps and internet platforms.

Online Savings Account Trends

Since online savings accounts sometimes offer better returns than traditional brick-and-mortar bank accounts, they have become more and more popular in recent years. The emergence of fintech firms and banks that operate exclusively online has completely changed the savings market by giving customers additional options and competitive interest rates.

Benefits of Savings Accounts Online

•   **Higher Interest Rates:** Online banks can provide higher interest rates on savings accounts because they often have lower overhead costs than traditional banks. Because of this, many looking for higher returns are finding online savings accounts to be an appealing choice.

•   **Convenience and accessibility:** Having an online savings account allows you to manage your money from any location with an internet connection. It's simple to set up automatic deposits, transfer money, and check balances with mobile apps and internet platforms.

Reduced costs: A lot of online banks provide savings accounts with a lower minimum balance requirement and no monthly maintenance costs. Customers may find it simpler to save now that they won't have to worry about fees deducted from their returns.

Online savings account challenges

Absence of Physical Branches: The lack of physical branches is a major disadvantage of online savings accounts. Although many customers don't mind, this restriction could be difficult for those who prefer in-person banking services.

Customer service: While online banks typically offer extensive phone, email, and chat support, some customers might prefer the more individualized care that physical banks offer.

Rate Fluctuations: Interest rates on online savings accounts fluctuate often, particularly in response to changes in the federal funds rate. It is important for savers to remain aware of changes in interest rates and to anticipate fluctuations in their returns.

Expert Analysis from Sources Like Greg McBride of Bank rate

Experts in finance, such as Greg McBride, chief financial analyst at Bankrate, provide insightful information about the savings environment and how changes in the Federal Reserve rate affect savings account rates. Key patterns and things to keep in mind when navigating the present economic climate are highlighted in McBride's research.

Perspectives on Present Savings Patterns

Competitive Rates: Online banks have been setting the standard for competitive savings rates, according to McBride. He points out that "top-yielding online savings account rates have made significant moves and are now paying as much as 5.5% — well above the rate of inflation." This suggests that internet banks are still offering savers appealing options despite economic uncertainty.

Rate Fluctuations: Interest rates on online savings accounts fluctuate often, particularly in response to changes in the federal funds rate. It is important for savers to remain aware of changes in interest rates and to anticipate fluctuations in their returns.

Inflation and Savings: McBride stresses that while assessing savings account rates, inflation must be taken into consideration. Although higher rates are advantageous, inflation should be factored into the real return on savings accounts. He clarifies that "earning a yield that exceeds inflation is a rare win for anyone building up a cash cushion."

Diversification: McBride suggests that investors and savers broaden their approaches to investing and saving. He advises looking at alternative investment vehicles, such as CDs, money market accounts, and even low-risk investment funds, for long-term growth, even though high-yield savings accounts are a fantastic choice for emergency funds and short-term savings.

Suggestions for Conservators

Shop Around for Rates: McBride advises customers to frequently assess the rates on savings accounts provided by various institutions. Because online banks are so competitive, transferring accounts or institutions frequently presents possibilities to obtain greater interest rates.

Remain Updated: Savers must stay up to date on Federal Reserve policy and economic developments. McBride advises keeping an eye on rate adjustments and financial news to make well-informed choices about where to store savings.

Strike a Balance between Accessibility and Returns: McBride advises against putting all of your funds in accounts that can have fines or restrictions on withdrawals, even though high-yield savings accounts are appealing. He suggests striking a balance between high-return accounts and those that make it simple to access money in case of emergency.

Make Use of Automatic Savings Tools: A lot of online banks provide tools, like rounding up debit card purchases and putting the difference into a savings account, to help with automatic savings. McBride advises making use of these resources to easily and regularly increase savings.

The interest rate policies of the Federal Reserve have a significant impact on how savings are distributed. Savings account yields are often higher in the case of higher interest rates, whereas lower rates are associated with lower returns. Finding appealing savings alternatives has been simpler for customers because of the proliferation of online savings accounts, which provide reasonable rates and a wider range of options.

Specialists such as Greg McBride provide insightful analysis of existing patterns and cost-saving techniques. Savers can make the most of their savings by maximizing their returns, comparing rates, and being educated about the shifting economic landscape. Anyone hoping to maximize their financial well-being and set a strong basis for the future must comprehend the relationship between savings account returns and Federal Reserve policy

Chapter 6

More Comprehensive Economic Consequences

Interest rate decisions made by the Federal Reserve have a significant impact on the whole economy. These choices affect consumer behavior, the state of the economy, and several important industries, such as home ownership, the vehicle industry, and student loan finance. Comprehending these consequences offers a valuable understanding of how monetary policy molds economic circumstances and influences daily existence. This chapter looks at how the Fed makes decisions that affect the state of the economy as a whole, the importance of consumer confidence and spending, and possible long-term repercussions on the housing market, auto industry, and finance for higher education.

The Effects of Fed Decisions on Global Economic Stability

The promotion of maximum employment and price stability is the Federal Reserve's core purpose; moderating long-term interest rates is its secondary objective. Determining interest rates is essential to accomplishing these goals and preserving general economic stability.

Impact on both deflation and inflation

Control of Inflation: The Fed usually seeks to control inflation by raising interest rates, which makes saving more appealing and borrowing costlier. Reduced corporate investment and consumer spending can result from higher rates, which can slow down the economy and lessen inflationary pressures. The Fed contributes to price stability, which is essential for economic stability, by controlling inflation.

Risks Associated with Deflation: On the other hand, when the Fed reduces interest rates, it does so to boost the economy during times of little or no inflation. Reduced interest rates lower borrowing costs, which promote investment and expenditure. By doing this, deflationary forces that can result in lower consumer spending and economic stagnation might be mitigated.

Impact on Job Creation and Economic Development

Employment Levels: By affecting hiring and company expansion, the Fed's interest rate policies can affect employment levels. Reduced interest rates make it more affordable for companies to borrow money, which enables them to invest in expansion and job creation. On the other hand, higher rates may result in less investment and slower employment expansion.

Economic Growth: The total growth of the economy is also impacted by interest rates. In general, lower rates boost economic activity by enticing company investment and consumer spending, which increases GDP growth. Higher rates, however, have the opposite effect of accelerating economic development by decreasing borrowing and expenditure.

Stability and the Financial Markets

Stock Market: The financial markets, which include the stock market, are subject to fluctuations in interest rates. As investors seek larger returns on their equity investments, lower interest rates may cause stock prices to rise. On the other hand, if borrowing costs rise and consumer spending declines, higher rates may result in lower stock prices.

Bond Market: Fed choices have an impact on the bond market as well. Bond prices usually decrease as rates rise and vice versa. This is because newly issued bonds with greater interest rates become more appealing than older bonds with lower rates.

Banking Sector: Interest rate fluctuations have an impact on the profitability of the banking sector. A larger difference between lending and borrowing rates can result from higher rates, which could increase bank profits. Higher default rates and financial instability, however, may result from rates rising too quickly.

The Significance of Consumer Spending and Confidence

Spending and consumer confidence are essential for economic growth and stability. Interest rate decisions made by the Fed have a big impact on consumer behavior, which impacts the economy as a whole.

Interest Rates Effect on Consumer Confidence

Perceived Economic Conditions: By indicating a favorable economic climate and stimulating borrowing and spending, lower interest rates can increase consumer confidence. Customers are more inclined to indulge in discretionary spending and make expensive purchases when they feel secure about their financial status.

Economic Uncertainty: On the other hand, increased interest rates may lead to economic uncertainty, which may erode customer confidence. Higher borrowing costs might result in lower consumer spending and a more cautious outlook, as does the possibility of slower economic growth.

impact on consumer spending

• Credit Costs: Shifts in interest rates have an impact on credit costs, which in turn affects consumer purchasing habits. Lower rates make borrowing less expensive for borrowers, which facilitates the financing of big purchases like homes and cars. Both economic growth and higher spending may result from this.

• Disposable Income: By making debt payments more expensive, higher interest rates can lower a person's disposable income. larger rates can result in larger monthly payments for borrowers with large debt loads, which would leave them with less money for discretionary expenditures.

Savings Behavior: Interest rates have an impact on saving behavior. By providing better returns on savings accounts and other financial products, higher rates can promote saving. Lower rates, on the other hand, can encourage spending over saving because the returns on savings aren't as appealing.

Possible Long-Term Impacts on Important Industries

The Federal Reserve's interest rate decisions impact many different areas of the economy. Making educated judgments and navigating changes can be made easier for stakeholders when they are aware of these possible long-term implications.

Property Market

House Prices and Affordability: Mortgage rates are directly impacted by interest rates, which in turn affect both. By lowering monthly mortgage payments, lower interest rates can make owning a home more affordable. This could raise demand for homes and drive up their prices. On the other hand, higher rates may make homes less affordable and slow down the housing market.

Housing Supply: The availability of homes may also be impacted by changes in borrowing rates. Reduced rates may encourage builders to invest in brand-new homes, increasing the supply of housing. However, builders might halt new projects if rising rates result in a decline in the market for housing.

Refinancing Activity: Interest rates have a direct impact on the volume of refinancing activity. Refinancing volume may rise in response to lower rates as homeowners want to take advantage of better terms. Increased interest rates may make homeowners less likely to refinance, which could lead to a decrease in refinancing activity.

Automobile Sector

Vehicle Sales: When it comes to auto financing, interest rates are important. Reduced interest rates can raise the affordability of auto loans, which will boost car sales. Conversely, higher rates have the potential to increase the cost of borrowing, which might damage the auto industry and potentially lower car sales.

Consumer Financing Options: To draw customers, automakers and dealerships frequently offer promotional financing rates. Lower interest rates from the Fed may result in more enticing financing options, which may persuade buyers to buy new cars. Reduced customer incentives and fewer promotional offerings may result from higher rates.

Auto Loan Delinquencies: One other factor influencing auto loan delinquencies is higher interest rates. Significant increases in borrowing prices could make it difficult for certain borrowers to make their vehicle loan payments, which would raise the delinquency rate and possibly put lenders in a difficult financial situation.

Finance for Education

Interest rates on student loans: Interest rates on student loans have a direct impact on how much borrowing money costs for schooling. Congress sets interest rates for federal student loans, while rates on private student loans are frequently variable and based on benchmarks that are impacted by Fed policy. While rising interest rates may put more financial strain on families and students, lower rates can lower the cost of borrowing money for schooling.

College Affordability: By affecting the cost of student loans, interest rate changes can affect how affordable education is. Elevated interest rates may result in escalated borrowing expenses, which might potentially reduce the affordability of college and escalate the amount of student debt.

Institutional Financing: Interest rates have an impact on how educational institutions are funded as well. Colleges and universities may find it more cheap to fund capital projects and infrastructure upgrades with lower rates. Higher rates may make borrowing more expensive for institutions, which may limit their capacity to make program and facility investments.

Interest rate decisions made by the Federal Reserve have a big impact on the economy as a whole. The Fed's actions are vital to preserving economic stability since they have an impact on financial markets, employment, inflation, and economic growth. Interest rate fluctuations have a significant impact on consumer confidence and spending; lower rates generally encourage these behaviors, while higher rates may have the opposite effect.

Interest rate fluctuations have a particularly big impact on important industries including housing, the auto industry, and funding for education. Refinancing activity, affordability, and home prices all have an impact on the housing market. Loan delinquencies, finance alternatives, and car sales are all impacted by the auto sector. Institutional funding, college affordability, and student loan costs all affect how much money is spent on education.

Gaining knowledge of these wider economic ramifications can help one better understand how monetary policy affects different facets of daily living and determines economic situations. Individuals and organizations may traverse the economic landscape and make wise financial decisions by remaining educated and adjusting to shifting interest rates.

Chapter 7

Getting Ready for Changes in Finances

Planning ahead and using strategic management are necessary for navigating financial changes, particularly those brought on by fluctuations in interest rates. Consumers experience shifting borrowing costs, shifting savings yields, and shifting effects on their overall financial health as the Federal Reserve modifies interest rates. This chapter highlights the value of financial planning and budgeting, offers helpful advice for navigating these changes, and lists resources and tools for successfully managing personal finances.

Useful Advice for Customers on Handling Rate Changes

Interest rate fluctuations can affect savings yields and loan payments, among other aspects of personal finance. Here are some useful advice for customers to properly handle these fluctuations:

Evaluate and Modify Your Spending Cap

Regularly review your budget: It is essential to regularly assess and modify your budget, particularly while interest rates are fluctuating. Examine your earnings, outgoings, and savings to see how interest rate fluctuations impact your financial circumstances.

Take Interest Rate Variations Into Account: Any changes to your credit card or loan interest rates should be reflected in an updated budget. Lower rates could free up extra cash, while higher rates might result in larger monthly payments.

Enhance Debt Control

Refinance High-Interest Debt: If interest rates drop, you might think about refinancing high-interest loans or credit card debt. Your monthly payments and interest rates may be lowered by refinancing.

Examine Transfers of Balance: For debt on credit cards, investigate balance transfer programs.

Review Investment and Savings Plans

Transfer to Higher-Yield Accounts: If interest rates rise, you should think about transferring your savings to higher-yielding accounts, including certificates of deposit (CDs) or high-yield savings accounts. You can increase your returns by doing this.

Invest Diversify: Various investments may be impacted differently by an environment with rising rates. Make sure your portfolio is diversified by including securities, equities, and real estate—all of which do well under different interest rate scenarios.

Make a Variable Rate Plan

Get Ready for Interest Rate Increases: If you have any variable-rate loans, make arrangements to increase your payments or put aside more money in case interest rates rise. If rates rise, this can help you handle larger payments.

Think About Fixed-Rate Products: To lock in lower rates and prevent future rises, think about choosing fixed-rate products for new credit or loans.

Keep an eye on financial metrics

Remain Up to Date: Pay attention to economic statistics including employment rates, inflation, and Federal Reserve announcements. Knowing these signs will enable you to predict interest rate fluctuations and modify your financial plans appropriately.

Adhere to Expert Analysis: Pay attention to the advice of economists and financial specialists. Their evaluations might offer helpful direction on how to react to

The Value of Budgeting and Financial Planning

Navigating the complexity of interest rate increases and maintaining long-term financial stability need effective budgeting and financial planning. The following explains their significance and how to include them in your financial plan:

Setting Budgetary Objectives

Establish Achievable Goals: The first step in financial planning is to establish attainable goals. These could be debt repayment, house ownership, or retirement savings. Goal-setting facilitates the development of a targeted financial plan and the monitoring of your advancement.

Set Prioritization for Your Goals: In your financial plan, list the priorities for the goals that are most essential to you. This guarantees that resources are allocated efficiently and that you move closer to your primary financial goals.

Making an All-Inclusive Budget

Monitor revenue and Expenses: A well-designed budget makes it easier to keep track of your revenue and outlays, giving you a clear understanding of your financial status. Keep an eye on your spending patterns to find places where you may reallocate or save money.

Set Aside Money for Savings and Debt payback: Make sure your budget leaves money set aside for both savings and debt payback. Maintaining your financial health requires paying off debt and setting aside a percentage of your salary for savings.

Establishing an Emergency Reserve

Save for Unexpected Expenses: An emergency fund acts as a safety net against unforeseen costs like auto or hospital bills. Three to six months' worth of living expenses should be saved and kept in a readily accessible account.

Modify for Interest Rate Changes: Examine and modify your emergency fund plan when interest rates are fluctuating. The earnings on your savings may be impacted by higher rates, so think about putting your emergency fund in a high-yield account.

Examining and Modifying Budgets

Frequent Reviews: Make sure your financial plan is still in line with your present objectives and situation by reviewing it on a regular basis. A change in employment or a large purchase are examples of life events that can need adjusting your strategy.

Adjust to Changes: Be adaptable and modify your financial strategy to account for variations in personal circumstances, interest rates, or the state of the economy. Making changes guarantees that your plan stays applicable and functional.

Resources and Tools for Taking Care of Personal Finances

Effective personal finance management calls for the utilization of a variety of instruments and resources. The following are some vital information and tools to assist you in adjusting to financial changes:

Tools for Budgeting: Apps for budgeting: You can track spending, keep an eye on your financial objectives, and establish and manage a budget with the aid of programs like Mint, YNAB (You Need A Budget), and PocketGuard. These apps have capabilities including budget management, spending classification, and financial analysis.

Spreadsheets: Using Google Sheets or Excel, you may create a budget spreadsheet if you're the more hands-on type. Spreadsheets make it possible to track income and expenses in great detail and with flexibility.

Tools for Debt Management: Debt Reduction Calculators: You can use online calculators to estimate the length of time it will take to pay off your debt and to build a plan for payback. Prioritizing the repayment of debt can be achieved with the help of calculators such as the Debt Avalanche or Snowball calculators.

Credit Score Monitoring: You may view your credit record and score using services like Credit Karma or Experian. Keeping an eye on your credit score enables you to efficiently manage your debt and remain informed about your creditworthiness.

Investment and Savings Instruments

High-Yield Savings Accounts: With competitive interest rates, online banks and financial institutions provide high-yield savings accounts. You can compare rates and identify the finest solutions for optimizing your savings with the aid of resources like Bankrate and NerdWallet.

Investment platforms: A variety of investment options, including stocks, bonds, and mutual funds, are available on platforms like Vanguard, Fidelity, and Robinhood. These platforms offer performance monitoring and investment management features.

Resources for Financial Planning

Financial Advisors: Seeking the advice of a financial advisor can help you develop a thorough financial strategy and offer tailored recommendations. Advisors can help with retirement planning, interest rate management, and investment strategies.

Educational tools: You may improve your financial literacy by using online tools including blogs, webinars, and courses on financial planning. Websites with useful information and instructional materials include Investopedia and the Financial Planning Association.

Savings and Emergency Fund Resources

Savings Calculators: To determine how much you should save for a particular purpose, such an emergency fund or a large purchase, use internet calculators. You can make smart plans with the aid of calculators such as the savings goal calculator and emergency fund calculator.

Automatic Savings Plans: A lot of banks have automatic savings plans that, on a regular basis, move a predetermined amount from your checking account to a savings account. This makes it easier and more consistent for you to grow your savings.

It takes a combination of realistic tactics, efficient financial planning, and the use of the right tools and resources to get ready for financial changes. You may handle interest rate swings and preserve financial stability by reviewing and modifying your budget, managing your debt more effectively, reassessing your savings and investing plans, and keeping up with current events.

Setting and accomplishing financial objectives, controlling spending, and laying a strong financial foundation all depend on financial planning and budgeting. You may manage your finances more successfully with the help of tools and services including investing platforms, debt management calculators, savings accounts, and budgeting apps.

You may better plan for changes in your money and achieve long-term financial success by managing your personal finances proactively and making use of the tools and resources that are available to you. You can manage changes in the economy, make wise decisions, and keep control of your financial destiny by remaining knowledgeable and flexible.

Chapter 8

Prospects for the Future

Because the Federal Reserve's actions on interest rates and monetary policy have a big impact on the economy, people and businesses who are planning their financial plans need to know what the future looks like. A wealth of information is available to help prepare for changes in monetary policy, including expert forecasts of future rate decreases, possible economic conditions, and several scenarios for different economic outcomes. This chapter examines forecasts from experts regarding rate decreases in the future, presents scenarios for various economic situations, and provides advice on getting ready for any changes in monetary policy.

Expert Forecasts for Upcoming Rate Reductions and Economic Situation

To predict future interest rate changes and economic conditions, experts examine a variety of economic indicators, historical data, and current trends. Their forecasts influence expectations and guide investment choices. The opinions of several experts regarding potential rate cuts and the state of the economy are summarized as follows:

Interest Rate Forecasts

Current Economic Indicators: In order to forecast future rate reduction, analysts keep a close eye on economic indicators like GDP growth, employment trends, and inflation rates. The Fed may think about cutting rates in order to boost economic activity if inflation stays over its objective or if growth in the economy considerably slows down. In contrast, the Fed may decide to keep rates the same or even raise them in order to restrain price increases if inflationary pressures continue.

Federal Reserve Statements: The FOMC members' and the Federal Reserve Chair's remarks and advice offer hints regarding potential future monetary policy. Based on the current state of the economy and their projections for it, Jerome Powell and other Fed officials frequently share their views on interest rate policy. Their remarks on employment, inflation, and economic growth affect market expectations for next rate adjustments.

Market Expectations: Bond yields and futures contracts on the financial markets also give clues about anticipated rate reductions. Bond yields, for instance, would drop and futures markets might indicate higher expectations for lower rates if market players predict a rate cut. Additional information on prospective rate adjustments in the future can be obtained by analyzing these market signals.

Economic Outlook and Situation

Trends in Inflation: To determine the possibility of further rate reductions, experts examine trends in inflation. The central bank may give controlling inflation a higher priority than promoting growth if inflation stays above the Fed's objective. In contrast, the Fed may think about lowering interest rates in order to boost the economy if inflation slows and reaches target levels.

Employment Data: Monetary policy actions are heavily influenced by the situation of the labor market. The Fed's decision-making process can be influenced by high employment and wage growth rates. The Fed may have more flexibility to change rates in order to promote other economic objectives if employment stays high.

Global Economic Factors: The Fed's choices are also influenced by global economic factors, such as trade conflicts, geopolitical developments, and global economic growth. Experts speculate on the potential effects of these variables on the monetary policy of the central bank as well as the state of the domestic economy.

Potential Courses of Economic Events

Depending on changes in interest rates, the state of the economy, and outside variables, several scenarios may come to pass. Knowing these possibilities enables people and organizations to get ready for many contingencies. Here are some crucial situations to think about:

Scenario 1: Ongoing Economic Growth Despite Rate Reductions In this scenario, the economy continues to develop at a strong rate and the Fed chooses to lower interest rates in order to boost the economy even more. Reduced rates may stimulate borrowing, company investment, and consumer spending all of which would support ongoing expansion.

Inflation: The Fed can cut rates without aggravating price hikes as long as inflation stays under control. Reduced borrowing costs benefit both consumers and businesses, which could result in increased economic activity and long-term growth.

Market Impact: Asset prices, such as those of stocks and real estate, may rise in response to lower interest rates. Companies might make more investments, and buyers might benefit from cheaper financing for large-ticket items.

Scenario 2: Rate reductions and an economic slowdown

Economic Growth: In this scenario, the Fed lowers interest rates in response to a slowdown in the economy in order to spur growth. There are a few reasons why the economy may be slowing down: lower consumer spending, less corporate investment, or external shocks.

Inflation: The Fed may be able to lower rates without raising serious concerns about inflation if it is contained or even dropping. Lower rates are intended to stimulate the economy and avert a more serious downturn.

Impact on the Market: When the economy is slowing down, rate reductions can assist and stabilize the financial markets. However, the fundamental reasons of the slowdown may determine how well rate decreases stimulate the economy.

Scenario 3: Higher rates and inflationary pressures

Economic Growth: In this scenario, the Fed raises rates in order to contain price increases since inflation stays above its target. Raising rates is intended to lower inflationary pressures by raising the cost of borrowing and slowing down the economy.

Inflation: The Fed is compelled to give price control a higher priority than growth stimulation due to persistent inflation. Increased rates may result in slower economic growth and higher borrowing costs, but they can also help control inflation.

Market Impact: Lower consumer spending and company investment may result from higher interest rates, which could have an effect on asset values and economic expansion. Investors may see volatility in the financial markets as they get used to increasing borrowing prices.

Scenario 4: Stagnant Economy with Uncertain Monetary Policy

Economic Growth: In this case, there is uncertainty over future monetary policy and the economy is either stagnating or growing very slowly. Given the conflicting economic indications, the Fed may be hesitant to alter interest rates significantly.

Inflation: The possibility of unpredictable or fluctuating inflation makes the Fed's decision-making process more difficult. The central bank may choose to take a wait-and-see stance, gradually changing interest rates in response to changing economic circumstances.

Market Impact: Financial markets may become volatile due to monetary policy uncertainty. Businesses and consumers might take a cautious stance, which would affect their choices about investments and expenditures.

Getting Ready for Possible Changes in Monetary Policy

Anticipating changes in monetary policy requires proactive management and strategic planning. The following are crucial tactics to assist people and companies in navigating possible changes:

Examine and Modify your financial plans

Update Your Financial Objectives: Take stock of your finances on a regular basis and make necessary adjustments in light of the state of the economy and projected shifts in interest rates. Make sure your objectives are attainable and reasonable in light of prospective changes in monetary policy.

Adapt Investment Strategies: Examine and modify your portfolio of investments to take advantage of any future interest rate fluctuations. To reduce the danger of losing money due to changes in borrowing rates and asset values, think about diversifying your investments.

Fortify Your Financial Hardiness

Create or Maintain an Emergency Fund: By creating or keeping an emergency fund, you can increase your financial resilience. Having a safety net might help you weather rough patches in the economy and deal with unforeseen costs.

Diminish High-Interest Debt: To strengthen your financial situation, concentrate on paying off high-interest debt. Debt reduction can ease financial strain and increase adaptability to fluctuations in interest rates.

Continue to Learn and Be Informed

Keep an eye on the economic indicators: Keep up with the major economic developments and factors that affect choices about interest rates. To be informed about possible policy changes, regularly monitor economic reports, Federal Reserve comments, and professional analysis.

Seek Professional Advice: To receive tailored advice on handling your finances in reaction to changes in monetary policy, speak with financial advisors or other specialists. Advisors can offer guidance on methods to improve your financial circumstances.

Make a Plan for Various Situations

Make Backup Plans: Make backup plans for a variety of economic eventualities, such as rate reductions, rate hikes, and slowdowns in the economy. By preparing for many scenarios, you may reduce financial risk and adapt to changing circumstances.

Examine Your Financial Flexibility: Determine how adaptable you are to changing situations and how flexible your finances are. Make sure you have the flexibility to modify your borrowing plans, investments, and budget as circumstances dictate.

Interest rate and economic forecasts for the future are important factors that influence financial planning and strategy. Professional forecasts offer insightful information on prospective rate reductions and economic results, assisting people and companies in being ready for various contingencies. Potential alterations in monetary policy can be efficiently navigated by developing financial resilience, recognizing different situations, and modifying financial strategies.

Essential tactics for handling financial shifts include keeping yourself informed, getting expert counsel, and making backup plans. You can more effectively manage economic swings and attain long-term financial stability by anticipating possible changes in monetary policy.

The Federal Reserve's actions have a significant influence on both the overall economy and the financial circumstances of specific individuals as it negotiates the difficulties of monetary policy. The decision-making process of the Federal Reserve, the impact of economic indicators, the significance of political neutrality, sector-specific effects, and future projections have all been covered in detail in this book. It is essential to comprehend these components in order to manage personal finances in a changing economic climate. The main ideas covered in the book are summarized here, along with the significance of comprehending the Fed's policies and the need for readers to continue being proactive and knowledgeable about managing their financial health.

Summary of Important Ideas
The Decision-Making Process of the Federal Reserve

The Federal Reserve's decision-making process is crucial in determining monetary policy. Interest rates are determined and modified by the Federal Reserve system, which includes the Federal Open Market Committee (FOMC) and the position of the Federal Reserve Chair. The Federal Reserve bases its judgments on economic indicators, including GDP growth, job data, and inflation. Fed Chair Jerome Powell's recent remarks emphasize the central bank's methodology for rate changes and its dedication to making apolitical, data-driven judgments.

The Rate Cut Decision and Economic Indicators

When deciding on monetary policy, the Fed heavily relies on economic information. GDP growth, employment figures, and inflation rates are examples of important indicators. The Fed's view on rate decreases is influenced by inflation rates, with a focus on striking a balance between price stability and economic growth. The state of the labor market can be inferred from employment figures, whereas GDP growth indicates the level of economic activity in general. The fact that inflation is declining but is still quite high suggests that rate adjustments should be made cautiously, striking a balance between promoting growth and reining in inflation.

The Federal Reserve and Political Neutrality

Sustaining the Federal Reserve's efficacy and reputation requires it to remain politically neutral. The historical background demonstrates the Fed's steadfast adherence to an apolitical position, eschewing actions impacted by electoral cycles or political pressure. The Fed is committed to making objective, fact-based judgments, as demonstrated by Jerome Powell's remarks. Knowing how the Fed operates in election years emphasizes how crucial it is to keep monetary policy and politics apart.

Possible Effect on Various Sectors

Changes in interest rates have varying effects on different industries, such as student loans, auto loans, mortgage rates, and credit card debt. Refinancing or negotiating lower rates are two ways for managing credit card debt in the face of fluctuating interest rates. Mortgage rates have an impact on refinancing and house purchases because of Fed policies. Affordability is impacted by auto loans and growing auto costs, while financial difficulties are brought on by private student loan variable rates. Comprehending these effects enables customers to make knowledgeable financial choices.

The Environment of Savings

Interest rates at the Federal Reserve directly affect savings account yields. Online savings account yields have moved significantly as a result of the Fed's modifications, helping savers during higher rate times. Trends in savings rates are highlighted by expert analysis, along with the significance of maximizing returns on savings techniques through optimization. Keeping up with these changes enables people to make wise choices about their savings.

The Wider Economic Consequences

Interest rate decisions made by the Fed are vital to the stability of the economy as a whole. They have an impact on spending, consumer confidence, and the long-term dynamics of a number of sectors, including mortgages, auto loans, and student loans. It is easier for people and businesses to predict and adjust to changes in the economic environment when they are aware of how these decisions affect economic stability.

Getting Ready for Cash Shifts

Strategic management and proactive planning are necessary to navigate financial changes. A few useful suggestions for customers are to review and modify investment and savings plans, as well as optimize debt management and budgeting. Achieving financial objectives and preserving stability need careful planning and budgeting. Effective financial management is supported by the use of tools and resources including investing platforms, debt management calculators, and budgeting apps.

Prospective Forecasts

Expert forecasts about future interest rate reductions and the state of the economy offer insightful information about possible outcomes. A range of scenarios, such as sustained economic growth, downturns, inflationary pressures, and stagnation, provide a framework for anticipating various economic changes. Updating financial planning, bolstering financial resilience, and remaining up to date on market expectations and economic indicators are all part of being ready for possible shifts.

Concluding Remarks on the Significance of Knowing the Fed's Decisions

Navigating the intricacies of personal finance and the larger economic landscape requires an understanding of the Federal Reserve's choices. Interest rates are impacted by the Fed's operations, which also have an impact on savings rates, borrowing costs, and general economic stability. Understanding how the Fed's actions affect many facets of financial management enables people and companies to make wise decisions and adjust to shifting circumstances.

Understanding the Fed's choices is crucial for reasons other than their direct financial effects. It entails understanding the larger economic backdrop, projecting future changes, and making strategic preparations for various contingencies. A well-informed approach to money management enables people to maximize savings, manage debt, adjust to interest rate fluctuations, and make plans for future financial objectives.

Motivation to Maintain Knowledge and Take Initiative in Personal Finance Management

Proactive and knowledgeable living is necessary for good personal finance management. Here are some tips to keep up a knowledgeable and proactive stance:

Keep abreast on financial news

Keep abreast on economic news on a regular basis, including information on market movements, economic indicators, and Federal Reserve decisions. Reliable sources of information about the state of the economy both now and in the future include economic reports, financial news websites, and Federal Reserve official announcements.

Get Knowledgeable About Money Management

By learning about personal finance, investment methods, and economic fundamentals, you may improve your financial literacy. Financial blogs, books, and online courses are a few examples of resources that can offer insightful information and support you in making wise financial decisions.

Keep an eye on and tweak your financial plan

Review and modify your financial plan on a regular basis in light of your unique situation and shifting market conditions. Remain adaptable and modify your plans in response to changes in market dynamics, economic data, and interest rates.

Speak with Financial Experts

Seek advice and help from financial planners or other specialists for individualized advice. Advisors can assist you in planning for long-term financial objectives, navigating difficult financial decisions, and creating strategies for handling interest rate fluctuations.

Make Use of Financial Resources and Tools

To properly manage your funds, make use of tools and services related to money management, such as investing platforms, savings calculators, and budgeting applications. You can maximize savings, keep tabs on spending, and make wise investment selections with the aid of these tools.

Make a variety of scenario plans

Create backup plans in case of various economic events, such as possible rate reductions, recessions, and pressure from inflation. You can avoid financial risks and respond to changing conditions more effectively by planning for several scenarios.

In summary

In conclusion, sound financial management requires an awareness of the Federal Reserve's actions and how they affect individual financial situations. The Fed's decision-making process, economic indicators, political neutrality, sector-specific repercussions, savings environments, larger economic ramifications, and future estimates have all been covered in this book in various ways. You may successfully manage financial changes and attain long-term financial stability by remaining knowledgeable, proactive, and adaptive.

As you proceed, keep in mind that managing your finances is a continual process that calls for alertness, flexibility, and never-ending education. You may make wise judgments and safeguard your financial future by keeping up with economic trends, learning about financial concepts, and making use of the tools and resources that are readily available.

www.ingramcontent.com/pod-product-compliance
Lightning Source LLC
Chambersburg PA
CBHW050324230526
45471CB00005B/2343